+L

1/99

Tropical Fish

Neal Pronek

Published in association with T.F.H. Publications, Inc.,
the world's largest and most respected publisher of pet literature

Chelsea House Publishers
Philadelphia

CONTENTS

Introduction 1
Classifying Fishes 9
The Livebearing Fishes 14
Family Cichlidae 32
The Characoids 44
The Anabantoids 50
Family Cyprinidae 53
The Catfishes 57
The Loaches 60
Miscellaneous Families 61

Fish: Keeping & Breeding in Captivity

Aquarium Setting Up
Siamese Fighting Fish
Catfish
Goldfish
Guppies
Marine Aquarium
Piranhas
Tropical Fish
Angelfish

Publisher's Note: All of the photographs in this book have been coated with FOTOGLAZE™ finish, a special lamination that imparts a new dimension of colorful gloss to the photographs.

Reinforced Library binding & Super-Highest Quality Boards

This edition ©1999 TFH Publications, Inc., 1 TFH Plaza, Neptune City, NJ 07753. This special library bound edition is made expressly for Main Line Book Company a division of Chelsea House Publishers.

Library of Congress Cataloging-in-Publication Data applied for
0-7910-5094-7

Library of Congress Cataloging-in-Publication Data

Pronek, Neal.
        Tropical fish / Neal Pronek.
                p. cm. — (fish and aquariums)
        Includes index.
        Summary: An identification guide to popular freshwater tropical fish, describing the different species and providing advice on which ones are good for beginners.
        ISBN 0-7910-5094-7 (hc)
        1. Tropical Fish--Juvenile literature. 2. Aquariums--Juvenile literature.
        (1. Tropical fish. 2. Aquariums.) I. Title. II. Series.
        SF457.25.P76 1998
        639.34'2—dc21   96-7568
                                                               CIP
                                                               AC

INTRODUCTION

This book is about tropical fishes, and it's basically for beginners. In it I'm going to talk about many of the different tropical fish species that are at least occasionally available at pet shops and aquarium specialty stores today. Part of what I say will relate to the best ways to keep certain species on the assumption that you've either already purchased them or might soon purchase them. Part, though, will relate strictly to specific recommendations about which fishes to get and which to avoid in the first place. Now, obviously, much of what I say in the latter regard is based purely on my personal tastes in tropicals, so the book is going to be biased in favor of some species and biased against others. Of course, if you stick with the tropical fish hobby for any length of time, you'll develop heroes and heavies of your own—and you'll tout newcomers onto your favorites and badmouth the ones you dislike, the same as I'm doing here.

Likes and dislikes aside, my major consideration in making specific recommendations will be to try to give you enough information to enable you to decide whether a given species will be a good one for you. That's for *you*, remember—which means that you have to do part of the work of deciding whether a particular species will be a wise choice. I can tell you, for example, that such and such is a bad fish to try to keep if you happen to have hard, alkaline water—but you're the one who has to determine whether you have such water. And I can tell you not to put two males of a certain species together in a small tank and give you some guidelines about differentiating the sexes in that species—but you're the one who'll have to decide whether you have two males or not. You have

PHOTO BY MP. AND C. PIEDNOIR.

The fishes you select for your first aquarium should be chosen with care. The angelfish and discus and tetras in this attractive aquarium get along peaceably enough, but that's not always the case among fishes.

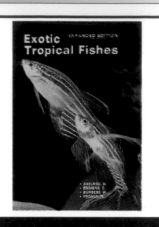

Exotic Tropical Fishes, **Expanded Edition is a 5 1/2 x 8 1/2 hardcover book with more than 1300 pages and over 1000 full-color photos. TFH style H-1028. The book contains full sections dealing with aquarium management, plant care and commercial breeding in addition to all the text describing individual species.**

plenty of help available to you in the form of larger books, such as *Exotic Tropical Fishes* and *Encyclopedia of Tropical Fishes*, as well as *Dr. Axelrod's Mini Atlas of Freshwater Aquarium Fishes*.

Essentially, I'm going to try to give you information that should make the keeping of tropicals more enjoyable because it helps you head off trouble before it begins. I think that one of the most important considerations along those lines is to let you know which fishes to avoid because they're psychos: there is not much fun to a hobby that has you spending most of your time counting corpses. And let me tell you, there are plenty of whackmeisters in the fish world; steer clear of them unless you're about half a nut yourself, in which case you might enjoy filling up your tanks with aquatic Ty Cobbs.

Keep in mind, though, that the behavior of fishes is not always predictable. Although it's true that fishes in the main are fairly brainless lowlifes that have enough sameness to them to make predicting their behavior worthwhile, they also have enough individual variation to throw off the accuracy of those predictions. Guppies, for example, are supposed to be very peaceful, non-aggressive fish that are perfect for the live-and-let-live, but I once had a female guppy that never seemed to let up on the other fishes in the tank, including some much bigger ones for which she was really no match....it appeared that she had them convinced that she was. This female guppy was living proof that the best defense is a good offense—she never stopped her picking, picking, picking. (And

Dr. Axelrod's Mini-Atlas of Tropical Freshwater Aquarium Fishes, **T.F.H. style H-1090, is a 5 1/2 x 8 1/2 hardcover book that contains 992 pages, more than 2200 full-color photos and a 256-page section treating aquarium management and fish care.**

DR. AXELROD'S MINI-
ATLAS
OF
FRESHWATER
AQUARIUM
FISHES
MINI EDITION

DR. HERBERT R.
AXELROD
DR. WARREN E.
BURGESS
DR. CLIFF W.
EMMENS

NEAL PRONEK
JERRY G. WALLS
RAY HUNZIKER

MORE THAN
1800 PHOTOS
IN
FULL COLOR

yes, she was really a guppy, not a gambusia.)

The same holds true for other areas of behavior, not just aggressiveness or the lack of it. I can tell you with complete assurance of being right, for instance, that male swordtails often jump out of their tanks unless those tanks are covered, but I'd never make a bet that any particular swordtail would eventually leap to his death, and I wouldn't try to give the lie to anyone who said that he never had a male swordtail jump, even though he had kept hundreds of them.

You get the point, I'm sure, so let's not beat it to death: individuals of a given tropical fish species are alike enough to make experience-based predictions possible, different enough to make them interesting.

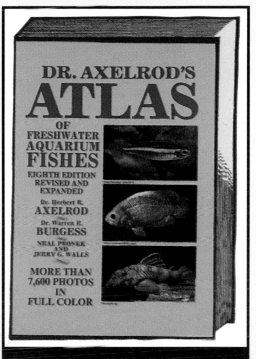

Dr. Axelrod's Atlas of Freshwater Aquarium Fishes, TFH style H-1077, is the world's largest identification guide to aquarium fishes. This 8 1/2 x 11 hardcover book contains more than 7600 full-color photos.

The sailfin molly is a good example of a popular aquarium species that is usually not a good species for a beginner. This male golden sailfin molly is very impressive with his dorsal fin fully unfurled, but mollies in general are very demanding of special conditions.

Those things are all specific do's and don'ts dealing with individual species and small groups of species. I'd like to pass along some specific do's and don'ts relating to the keeping of tropicals in general—information you can put to good use no matter which fishes you keep.

1.   Make frequent partial changes of the water. Fishes excrete into the water in which they live, and when water evaporates (which happens to be a continuous process in an aquarium, even a covered aquarium) it evaporates in pure form, leaving behind all of the impurities that might have been mixed into it. Therefore impurities in a container of standing water— and your tank is a container of standing water regardless of how powerful your filtration/aeration equipment is—tend to become concentrated as the water gets older. Therefore the water continuously deteriorates over the course of time, until you eventually reach a point at which your tank

Filtration of some type should be used in the aquarium, because although filtration devices can't replace the hobbyist entirely, they definitely are of value. These are undergravel filters, available in different sizes to fit different tank sizes. Your dealer should be able to give you sensible guidance about the filtration requirements of your aquarium.

becomes a sort of decorative cesspool. The best way to prevent your aquarium from becoming a sewer is to change part of the water at regular intervals. Changing 15% of the water twice a week is not too much, changing 10% once a week is too little, but it's a lot better than no change at all. In making the changes, you can take water right from the tap if your water supply hasn't been treated with

Here is a fish that looks innocent enough to be chosen by a beginner attracted by its sinuous grace and the colorful black-bordered line along its flanks: a young _Channa micropeltes_, the redlined snakehead. But it's a murderous beast and has the potential for quickly becoming far too large by home aquarium standards.

The Australian rainbowfish *Melanotaenia maccullochi* is an example of one of the many peaceful and relatively undemanding species that are widely available to beginning aquarists.

chloramine. If it has, you should use a chlorine/chloramine neutralizer to treat the new water. Good neutralizing products are available. Just be sure that the new water you use is the same temperature as, or a few degrees warmer than, the water you take out. If you don't want to do the changing of the water yourself, you can buy an automatic water-changing device in an aquarium store; however you choose to do it, get it done. It really is the best

Aquarium water has a number of chemical properties that greatly affect the health of the fishes in it. Its pH (relative acidity/alkalinity), hardness, and nitrate/nitrite content are among the important properties that the hobbyist can easily test for through the use of test kits available at pet shops.

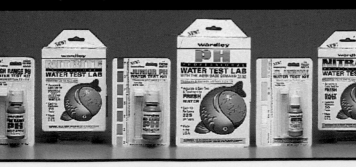

Newly hatched larvae of the marine crustacean *Artemia salina* are the mainstay food for baby tropical fishes and are relished by many small adult fishes as well. Pet shops and tropical fish specialty stores offer all of the equipment and supplies—including, of course, the brine shrimp eggs themselves—needed by hobbyists to produce their own live food.

Automatic water-changing devices can make the necessary job of making regular partial water changes easier and less subject to mess and spillage.

thing you can do for your fishes. They'll grow better...look better...feel better and spawn better if kept in tanks in which portions of the water are regularly replaced with fresh new water—so you'll certainly enjoy them more.

2. Feed some live foods occasionally. Okay, live foods aren't always easy to obtain, and they're comparatively expensive when you can get them. But they're fine treats for your aquarium inmates, and you'll really enjoy yourself watching your fishes eat them. Don't cheat yourself out of the experience of watching hungry fishes in your tank tear into a cupful of live adult brine shrimp or some such. If you can't get any live foods, at least try some frozen foods.

Other points of information that

Frozen foods in a wide range of different basic contents, from 100% animal-based through 100% vegetable-based, are available for both freshwater and marine aquarium fishes, so hobbyists can cater to the requirements of a particular species or group of species as well as provide a very varied diet to non-picky eaters.

experiences as a fishkeeper. They're not the type of data that you should pick up bit by bit over the course of time as you acquire veteran status as a tropical fish hobbyist; they should be pointed out to you, because they're not normally learned as a result of experimentation. You could keep mollies for forty years, for instance, without learning that they do best with salt in their water; it's the kind of thing someone else has to tell you.

I've been keeping fishes for about fifty years myself, and I know that I've learned much more from what people have told me than from what I've been able to observe. Some things are just not worth learning if the only way you can learn them is by direct observation alone. As a purely practical

could be useful to you in deciding which fishes to get and which to stay away from include such things as special foods required (most tropicals that you'll see being offered for sale will live on a diet of dried or frozen foods alone, but a few require live offerings), special tank decorations required (some fishes are going to look and feel about 400% better if you give them what they need in their tanks than if you had ignored their requirements), special water qualities required (which usually has to do with temperature, hardness/softness and acidity/ alkalinity ratios but can include such things as salt content). These are things that, for the most part, you're not going to learn solely from your own

Encyclopedia of Tropical Fishes basically is a book about how to breed aquarium fishes. TFH style H-905, it's a 5 1/2 x 8 1/2 hardcover book of over 600 pages.

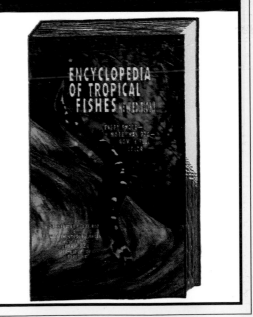

consideration, it's a lot quicker and easier to learn how a fish breeds by looking up its breeding habits in a book than it is to keep yourself in the dark until you get a chance to see the fish spawn in your tank. Sure, observing the actual spawning will show you much more of the fine points of the action and convey a much finer feel for what's going on than a book ever could—but if you didn't know beforehand how the fish is supposed to spawn you

might never have had a chance to observe the mating in the first place.

That's basically what I'm going to try to do in this book. I'm going to try to tell you things about the different fish species that you have a chance to buy, things that you should take into consideration before bringing the fishes home with you. It's a lot easier on everybody—especially the fishes—if you know what you're doing.

Something else we'll be covering is the reproductive patterns of the fishes discussed. Although most people who start in the tropical fish hobby never breed even one egglaying species, learning about the breeding habits of the fishes they own is important to them. They might never make a serious effort to breed anything in their tanks, but the potential is there—and it's fascinating.

Observing the breeding habits of your fishes is one of the most entertaining rewards offered by the tropical fish hobby, and many popular tropical fish species spawn readily under good aquarium conditions. The photo above shows fry of the Siamese fighting fish, *Betta splendens*, grouped under the bubblenest into which they were deposited as eggs. Below a pair of *Laetacara curviceps*, one of the South American cichlid species, are seen hovering over the clutch of eggs they have deposited on a rounded rock.

PHOTOS BY R. ZUKAL.

CLASSIFYING FISHES

All animals—and fishes are animals in the same sense that birds, mammals, insects and worms are animals, in that they're not plants or minerals—are categorized into different types. The animals are grouped according to likenesses and differences that appeal to the people who do the classifying as being sensible points of departure. The points of departure are physical characteristics that usually are easily observable and therefore verifiable in terms of their presence or absence: a bird has feathers, but a mammal doesn't; an insect has legs, but a snail doesn't; these three fishes have scales, but that one doesn't.

It is assumed by the classifiers that all of the animals are more or less related, and it is further assumed that the points of departure have significance in determining the degree of closeness of relationship. The classification of animals according to their supposed relationships is called taxonomy, and the people who do the classifying are called taxonomists or systematists. Their work is vital to many other areas of biological study, if for no other reason than that it facilitates communication by providing generally agreed-upon identifications: you can't tell the players without a scorecard. Where animals are concerned, the taxonomists make the scorecards, and their tools are the taxa (categories) they devise.

Like all other animals, fishes are classified into big, very inclusive groups that are broken down into smaller, less inclusive groups, with the smaller groups being broken down into yet smaller and less inclusive groups. Ranged in the order of descending inclusion, for example, for fishes the biggest and most inclusive group would be the kingdom Animalia, which contains all animals. Then would come the phylum; for fishes it would be the phylum Vertebrata, which contains all animals with backbones. Less inclusive would be the next taxon,

Xenomystus nigri, an African knife fish, doesn't have the same general shape that we usually associate with aquarium (and other) fishes, but it's a full-fledged member of the class Osteichthyes (in this case order Osteoglossiformes, family Notopteridae) nevertheless.

the class, which for aquarium fishes would be the class Osteichthyes, the bony fishes (in contradistinction to the cartilaginous fishes, the sharks and rays). Continuing in descending order of inclusiveness, the remaining taxa would be the order, the family, the genus and the species. Things aren't always as clear-cut as the taxonomists would like them to be, so in certain areas they've had to set up intermediate taxa in the form of superorders and subfamilies, subgenera and subspecies and suchlike to make distinctions between each group clearer.

The four taxa that we'll be concerned with in this book are the order, the family, the genus and the species. We'll be concerned with them in only the most elemental sense, because all we'll be doing is just throwing the names around. But still you'll be able to see from the photos in the book what the taxonomists are basically driving at: the fishes in a given family look as if they are related; they at least generally look more like each other than they look like fishes from other families.

Five orders (the Cypriniformes, the Characiformes, the Siluriformes, the Cyprino-dontiformes and the Perciformes) comprise probably 95% of the fishes in the freshwater aquarium hobby. The remaining 5% are spread over another four or five orders. Just for the record, here are four orders that contain the bulk of aquarium fishes, with the listings of the best-known families of aquarium fishes that each order contains:

Hyphessobrycon herbertaxelrodi, the black neon tetra, one of the attractive and peaceable small tetra species commonly seen in aquarium shops.

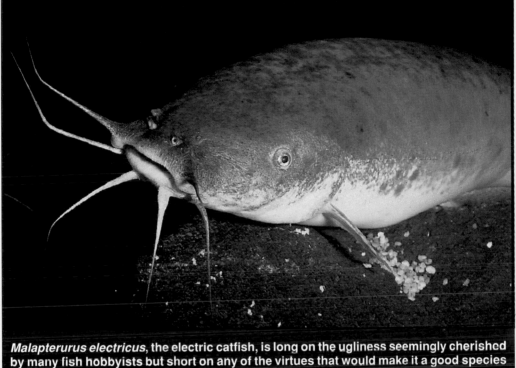

PHOTO BY KEN LUCAS.

Malapterurus electricus, the electric catfish, is long on the ugliness seemingly cherished by many fish hobbyists but short on any of the virtues that would make it a good species for beginners.

• Characiformes contains all of the many small "tetras" such as the cardinal tetra, the neon tetra and the lemon tetra of the family Characidae, (which incudes, among others, the subfamily Serrasalminae (the piranhas), hatchetfishes (family Gasteropelicidae), and the pencilfishes (family Lebiasiniadae).

• Cypriniformes includes all of the carp-like fishes such as the barbs, rasboras and danios, as well as (again among others) the loaches.

• Siluriformes contains numerous families of catfishes, including a great diversity of aquarium fishes.

• Cyprinodontiformes contains the livebearers as well as the killifishes and a few other families.

• Perciformes contains the cichlids (such as the angelfish) and the anabantoids (such as all of the gouramies and the Siamese fighting fish); it also contains the spiny eels.

Most families contain a number of genera, but some families have only one. Likewise, most genera contain more than one species, but some contain only one.

It's possible, then, for a family to contain only one species. That's an unusual situation, but it can occur; among aquarium fishes, an example of a family containing

A male *Badis badis,* one of the species that has a family all to itself. Never a popular fish even though at its best it (breeding males, at least) is much more handsome than some of the dwarf cichlid species with which it's often confused, *Badis badis* has one big drawback as an aquarium fish: it won't eat anything but living foods. The male shown here is in breeding color but not at the peak of its best breeding dress.

only one species is the family Badidae, which contains *Badis badis*, the chameleon fish.

You'll have noticed from even the very limited amount of taxonomy presented here that there are certain conventions observed in presenting the names of the different taxa. The names of all of the orders, for instance, end in —iformes, the suborders in —ei and the families in —idae. Also, the names of genera and species are given in *italic* type, whereas all the taxa above the genus are kept in regular type. Additionally, the first letter in the generic name is capitalized, whereas the first letter of a specific name is not, even if the specific name is coined from a proper name, such as a person's name or a geographical place name.

In effect, the generic and specific names applied to a particular fish *are* the name of the fish. Some tropical fish hobbyists take pleasure from learning and using the names of not only the fishes they own but also the ones they've only read about or seen in dealers' tanks. They (and who doesn't) may mangle the pronunciation of the names and may have no idea what they mean, but they have at least a partial grip on them. Other hobbyists deliberately ignore the scientific names, insisting on being provided with "common" names instead. I think the people in the latter group are missing out on a nice little slice of the hobby's charm, and they're giving it up for no good reason. The names aren't that tough to master, as witness the fact that some who feel queasy about spitting out an occasional piscine generic name will blithely tell you how their chrysanthemums and rhododendrons are doing.

The fishes get their names, incidentally, from the taxonomists, who put names on fishes that they think have never been described and named before. Certain internationally agreed-upon rules and a certain etiquette govern the publication of scientific papers naming new species, but essentially it's a process of describing what is hoped to be a new-to-science fish and showing how it differs from known species it's supposed to be most closely related to. You'll often see the name of the fish's describer (its "author") following the name of the fish when the fish's name is referred to in print; often the year of the description is also listed. Sometimes the describer's name is set within parentheses; the appearance of the parentheses signifies that the generic name given for the fish is not the one originally applied by the person whose name appears within those parentheses. A plain "L" or "L." after a name is an abbreviation for Linnaeus, which is the Latinized version of the surname of Karl von Linne, the 18th century biologist who was most instrumental in having the system of coupling a generic and specific word-pair accepted as the name by which naturalists would recognize a particular animal. The system has worked well for over 200 years now.

A pair (male is the upper fish) of the golden color phase of the lyretail, *Aphyosemion australe*. Beautiful, easy to keep and easy to breed — but still, like the other killifishes, never really a popular species.

THE LIVEBEARING FISHES

The fishes of the family Poeciliidae are among the most popular of all aquarium fishes. The family includes the guppy, the mollies, the platies, the swordtails and a few others, a group not very rich in species but definitely heavily represented in fish hobbyists' tanks. One of the livebearing species usually is the first type of fish kept by a beginner, and that's good, because most of the livebearers are hardy, interesting, peaceable aquarium inhabitants. But no doubt the main charm of the livebearers among beginning hobbyists is the relative ease with which their keeper can obtain from them babies that are easy to raise. Most beginning hobbyists, especially young beginning hobbyists, are fascinated by the idea of having their fishes reproduce themselves in their tanks, and once those babies are produced they'll do everything they can to raise them to maturity. The livebearing fishes make it easy for aquarists both ways: they're easy to breed and also very easy to raise—or at least it's much easier to breed and raise them than any of the egglaying species. Really, a good deal of the growth of the aquarium hobby in popularity results from the ease of handling and raising livebearing species; without them, there would have been many more beginners who would have dropped out of fishkeeping because it bored them. The livebearers kept them in.

The difference between livebearers and egglayers is that baby livebearers are delivered fully formed and ready to swim and go about their business. They don't have to hatch out of eggs or anything like that; they're on their way the minute they're born. To the fishkeeper, this is a tremendous advantage when it

PHOTO BY DR. HERBERT R. AXELROD.

A male sphenops molly, *Poecilia sphenops;* sphenops mollies are less demanding of special water conditions than the sailfin mollies. Note the gonopodium, fairly typical of the intromittent organ of males of the fishes in the family Poeciliidae, which contains all of the truly popular livebearing aquarium fish species.

comes to raising the babies. It means, for one thing, that he really has babies, not just eggs that might or might not hatch into fry that might or might not starve to death very quickly because he can't provide them with food they can eat. You see, getting the fish to breed usually isn't the tricky part of fish-breeding. Feeding the fry is the tricky part, and that's where the livebearers have it all over the egglayers.

Another thing that makes livebearers easier to breed is that you'll have no problem distinguishing the sexes, which with many egglayers is not the case at all. Adult male livebearers possess a rod-shaped copulatory organ situated at about the midpoint of the bottom of the body; at more or less the same spot, adult females have a regular fan-shaped fin. Additionally, the males and females are shaped

PHOTO BY H. J. RICHTER.

A male variatus platy, *Xiphophorus variatus,* of the hi-fin form in which the dorsal fin is greatly elongated, to the degree that it often is draped down over the body of the fish, as here.

Free-swimming egglayer fry almost always demand minute living foods that the hobbyist has to culture himself, but baby livebearers can take whatever their parents have been eating, just reduced in size. They'll eagerly accept, and will thrive on, stuff you can shake out of a can, whereas many hungry egglayer babies on the prowl would die before they'd accept a substitute for living prey to ingest.

differently. In guppies and swordtails, differences in body shape between the sexes are pronounced to the degree that the sexes are immediately recognizable without recourse to scrutiny for presence or absence of a gonopodium, and in the platies and mollies, the males and females convey a somewhat different over-all look even though the basic body structure remains the same.

Another thing that makes the common livebearers easier to breed is that with them you don't even have to have both sexes in the tank to produce young. All you need is a pregnant female. Moreover, the female need not even have been exposed to a male for months before the birth, because once she's been impregnated she stays impregnated for more than one gestation period. An impregnated female guppy, molly, platy or

of the water. At about 78° F, the interval between births will be about a month; at lower temperatures, the interval can increase to three or four months. The number of young produced at one birth will range from just ten or so for young females at their first delivery to over a hundred for healthy females at their peak.

Newborn livebearers have to be protected against being eaten by their parents and other fishes. The babies are fairly adept at

PHOTO BY AARON NORMAN.

Corydoras acutus, one of the inoffensive little South American catfish species often kept by aquarists as "scavengers." Unlike the vast majority of other aquarium fishes, the *Corydoras* catfishes in the main are safe to maintain in the same tank as baby livebearers.

swordtail should produce at least two or three batches of offspring from just one insemination.

The length of time between each litter of babies depends primarily on the general quality of health of the mother and the temperature

hiding out among plants, especially bushy floating plants, real or artificial, but they're dead meat if kept in the same tank as a skilled hunter like an angelfish. Some adult fishes (*Corydoras* catfishes are an example) will

A pair of sailfin mollies, *Poecilia velifera.* The male of this pair is the fish in which the "sail" fin is much more highly developed than it is in the female.

mostly ignore baby livebearers, some (bettas come to mind) will make attempts at them but don't usually follow up beyond a few unsuccessful lunges, and some (a number of the killies) seem eager to eat them but unable to hunt them down unless the babies swim right past their mouths; out

BREEDING LIVEBEARERS

Breeding livebearers consists essentially of putting a male and a female into the tank together and then waiting while the female gets fatter and fatter; when it appears that her abdominal region can't take any more stretching, she'll have her babies. In fact, it will be

This closeup of the midsection of a female *Xenotoca eiseni* shows the bulge-bellied heaviness often exhibited by female livebearers. *Xenotoca* is not one of the popular and commonly available livebearing species; it's in a different family from the poecilids, the family Goodeidae.

of sight, out of mind. Baby-saving devices can be used to save as many as possible at birth, and it's best to keep the babies separate from all potential predators, including their own parents, until they put on enough size to prevent their being swallowed. Just don't underestimate the maw-stretching capacity of a hungry tankmate—a hungry fish doesn't have to be very big to be able to cram in a baby livebearer, even if the baby has a few months' growth under its belt.

hard for you to buy a pair of livebearers in which the female isn't already pregnant, so don't worry about having to coax your fishes into mating rituals. To get them to produce, all you have to do is keep them alive. (Keep in mind, now, that we're talking about the livebearers that you normally see in dealers' tanks, not the really gussied-up long-finned, veiltailed and lyretailed strains of swordtails, platies and mollies. Some of the highly developed livebearers are not in the least easy to breed; in the hands of anyone but experienced specialists, in fact, many of the latter are literally sterile.

Saving the babies is a different story. You have to do a little bit of work there. Aquarium stores sell a number of devices intended to save baby livebearers from being eaten. If you don't want to use any of them, just put the female (don't move her if it's very close to the time for her to drop the young) into a small tank by herself and stock the tank heavily with bushy plants in which the babies can hide. Remove the female from the tank after the babies are born and feed the babies well while keeping them at about 78°F. They'll grow quickly and start producing babies of their own in three months or so, often even earlier. Incidentally, when you remove the female from the tank in which she dropped the young, don't put her right back into the main tank, as she can use a little undisturbed rest.

Guppies

Guppies are nice. They usually don't bother anyone, they have nice colors, and they provide plenty of action in the tank. Today's guppies are bigger and better than ever before, and the females are getting more colorful all the time. Oddly enough, guppy breeders' insistence on uniformity from fish to fish in certain show categories is starting to produce

A male red delta guppy. The reason for the appellation red is obvious, and the "delta" part of the name refers to the size and angulation of the tail fin. This is a very highly developed exhibit-quality fish.

PHOTO BY STAN SHUBEL

PHOTO BY H. J. RICHTER.

The colors on this top-sword guppy are close to the colors (and the color pattern) of many wild-type male guppies, especially as to the pinkish blotches.

an over-all sameness in a species that was once lauded for its lack of uniformity in the colors of the males.

Guppies come in many different basic colors and color patterns, and there are even a few different tail types. Regardless of color or tail type, though—and this is a point that applies to the other species with many different color varieties and shapes, such as goldfish—all guppies are of one species. The currently accepted scientific name of the guppy is *Poecilia reticulata*; wild guppies originated in northern South America and off-lying islands, but today they are found wild in many other places, having been introduced for their usefulness in eating mosquito larvae, thereby helping to control mosquito-spread diseases such as malaria.

Today's fancy guppies are very impressive. Both the males and the females are much larger and more colorful than they were even just ten years ago, at which time they had already far surpassed their progenitors. Female fancy guppies of some strains now show definite flushes of color; they no longer are an over-all fishy brownish gray. They also have a much more highly developed finnage than the females of old. And the males keep getting bigger and bigger, with wider and wider tails. Additionally, the intensity of color in the males—especially in the red strains—leaves little room for improvement.

Platies

There are two species of popular livebearing fishes that have "platy" in their common names. One is *Xiphophorus maculatus*, the platy, also called "moon" and "platy moon"; pregnant females are called "full moons," and platies raised in Florida ponds are called "moons over Miami." (Nah.) The other is *Xiphophorus variatus*, the variatus platy, also called the platy variatus. The two species look fairly much alike, but *X. maculatus* is a chunkier, higher-bodied fish than *X. variatus*. Once you've seen good examples of each species you'll have no trouble telling them apart. There have been many cross-breedings between the two species over the years, though (and also between them and the swordtail), so just about any platy you run across will carry a mixture of genetic material from more than one *Xiphophorus* species, even if it is readily typed as to a particular species by its looks.

Both platy species are peaceful, non-troublemaking fishes. Males of both species, but especially *X. variatus*, engage in occasional squabbles with or without females in their tank, but they don't deal out steady punishment to one another or to any other fishes. Females are basically the same way, although you occasionally run into a mean female who tries

These three guppies, two males and a heavily pregnant female, constitute a trio numerically but not in the parlance of the aquarium trade, where a trio is two females and one male.

PHOTO BY A. ROTH

PHOTO BY H. J. RICHTER.

A male blue variatus platy, pretty close in coloration to the type of platy variatus males available in much greater number before the advent of newer color varieties such as the marigolds and sunsets.

This male red tuxedo wears his tuxedo (the black overlying his sides) with almost as much class as Fred Astaire wore his.

PHOTO BY H. J. RICHTER.

A male sunset variatus platy.

to make life miserable for every other livebearer in her tank.

Platies come in many different colors and patterns, with *X. maculatus* being available in a greater variety than *X. variatus*. To me the old tried-and-true solid golds, blues and reds (in *X. maculatus*) and blues and marigolds (in *X. variatus*) are the prettiest, but some of the newer varieties are strikingly colorful.

Since the mid-1960s, platies, like the swordtails, have been available in long-finned forms in which the fins, especially the dorsal, are extended far past their normal size. Some of these new

This female gold platy has a high dorsal fin and a clearly delineated "Mickey Mouse" pattern in the tail area.

PHOTO BY H. J. RICHTER.

The male is the lower fish in this pair of gold platies, which usually would be sold as "comets" because of the black edges to the upper and lower parts of the tail.

PHOTO BY A. ROTH.

A pair of marigold variatus platies, female above.

strains are silly-looking the way their fins droop and drag, but others are very showy indeed. The long-finned varieties usually are more expensive than their plainer cousins, and they are much less reliable as breeding stock.

Swordtails

In the same genus as the platies is the swordtail, *Xiphophorus helleri*. The platies and swordtails interbreed easily, to the point that many strains of both species have been heavily hybridized, with consequent erosion of the differences between them. Still, it is very simple to distinguish between a platy and a swordtail if the fishes you use for comparison are at all true to their original type.

Good male swordtails are the designer models among the livebearers, long and low and sleek-looking in contrast to their chunky relatives and most other tropicals. The "sword" extending from the tail of a nicely shaped male is a truly distinctive feature, a touch of pure elegance. Even the most jaded hobbyist can summon up enthusiasm for a tankful of good swordtail males. They are classy fish.

Like the platies, swordtails come in many colors. The basic colors are green and two forms of red, brick red and velvet red, but those old standbys now coexist with golds, albinos, pineapples and many others. Again like the platies, swordtails also exist in long-finned forms. Possibly because they are over-all bigger and more streamlined, swordtails seem to benefit more

The colors of many aquarium fishes are best appreciated under lighting that glances off the sides of the fish in such a way as to highlight the beautiful spanglings and iridescences they often possess, like the turquoise spanglings along the sides of the male in this pair of black swordtails. The miserable stumpy sword is common in swordtails of this color variety.

PHOTO BY R. ZUKAL

PHOTO BY A. ROTH.

The female of this pair of albino swordtails delivered a batch of young not long before this photo was taken, so she shows no fullness at all.

The male of this pair of lyretailed hi-fin swordtail sports a magnificent tail. The color is standard for what normally are sold as brick-red swordtails.

in appearance than do the platies from all of the fin-lengthening and veiltailing and lyretailing they've been through—but that's for you to judge.

Swordtails (the males more so than the females) are jumpers, so keep a tank housing swordtails well covered. A thick layer of floating plants will tend to cut down on the aerial acrobatics, but don't count on it as a sure cure.

The male of this pair of green swordtails—which show colors very close to those of wild swordtail stock—has a decent but not a great sword.

Mollies showing the coloration that this male *Poecilia sphenops* shows generally are sold under the name "gold dust mollies". The greater the preponderance of yellow in the color of the fish, the goldier the name becomes, with some nearly purely yellow specimens going under the name "24 karat gold dust mollies."

Mollies

Mollies are popular even though the most desirable of them are much less hardy than the other common livebearers. Perhaps the relative ease of maintenance of some of the mollies—such as the sphenops molly, *Poecilia sphenops*—makes potential purchasers of the larger and harder to maintain sailfin mollies, *Poecilia velifera* and *Poecilia latipinna*, think that they'll have the same level of success with the sailfins that they did with the sphenops. Unfortunately, it usually doesn't work out that way.

Easy to keep or tough to keep, mollies are commonly offered for sale. They come in degrees of black (ranging from a beautiful velvety solid black down to the miserable blotchiness of a "marble" molly), golden, albino, chocolate and even reddish-orange colors, with and without modified finnage in the form of lyretails and veiltails.

At their best, sailfin mollies are magnificent—big, bold, showy, colorful, vigor-radiating fish in which the males can unfurl an enormous banner of a dorsal fin and ripple it in its majesty while posing across a female's, or a rival male's, path. At their worst, they're shaky, wobbly, fin-clamped zeros huddled in a corner waiting to die of some piscine pip. If you ever want to know what a tropical fish hobbyist means when he says a fish has the shimmies, just watch a sick molly.

Mollies like warm water and can't stand chilling at all, so make sure they're given continuous warmth of no less than 72°F, with 78°F being ideal. They are reputed to need more vegetable matter in their diet than other livebearers require, and special dry foods with high vegetable contents are available for them.

Baby mollies are bigger and bulkier than other livebearers, but they're also slower-moving and less active. Luckily for them, their parents are less likely to eat them than other livebearer parents are to eat their own young. No female livebearer benefits from being netted and moved when she's heavy with young, but female mollies seem to suffer most from such treatment. Also, female mollies are the least amenable to being enclosed in livebearer breeding traps; they're much better off in a heavily planted tank.

All of the mollies do better with some sea salt (half a teaspoonful per gallon for sphenops and Yucatan sailfin mollies, a full teaspoon for regular sailfins) in their water, which is one reason they do best if kept in tanks by themselves, not mixed in with other species.

The common name molly, often given as mollie, comes from an old name for the genus: *Mollienesia*, which in turn was derived from the name of the French naturalist Frederic Mollien.

My advice: stay away from the mollies, at least the sailfins, until you've gotten some experience in the hobby and have developed a feel for giving fishes what they need; lay off mollies until you know what you're doing. But if you still want them after you've mastered the fundamentals, get yourself a couple of pairs or trios of the biggest and best sailfins around and let them put on a permanent show for you.

Misshapen, unquestionably, but mollies of this type (called "balloon" mollies) have been popular for years and are well entrenched on the aquarium scene.

PHOTO BY H. J. RICHTER.

Both male (upper fish) and female of this pair of black mollies exhibit a nice sooty black over the entire body.

FAMILY CICHLIDAE

The fishes of the family Cichlidae cover a lot of ground geographically, visually and behaviorally. The family includes some small and eminently inoffensive species like the ram as well as some voracious behemoths like the oscar and some downright sickos like the jewel fish. Two basic spawning patterns are used: egg-sticking and mouthbrooding; each pattern has many variations, and both are fascinating to observe. All in all, you probably could easily get a consensus that the cichlids are the most interesting fishes to watch spawn and care for their young. The cichlids, in fact, are almost the only aquarium species that tend their young in the sense of keeping the fry with them as a "family." Even the bubblenesting anabantoids, which go through an elaborate spawning routine and then tend the eggs for at least a few days afterward, don't come anywhere near the cichlids in the total number of fish-hours devoted to fry care. Even if you forget spawning patterns and fry care completely, you'd still probably be able to get a consensus that the cichlids are the most interesting aquarium fishes, because they are.

Cichlids on the whole exhibit more deliberateness in their actions; they seem to know more about what they're doing and why they're doing it than fishes of other families do. They show some

purpose behind their actions, whereas most of the others just flit and float around. Many tropical fish hobbyists are attracted to the cichlids because of their interesting behavior—which, incidentally, is as evident in the smallest members of the family as it is in the big boys—and become cichlid specialists, keeping no other species except what they might raise as food for their always-hungry favorites.

Traditionally almost all of the cichlids in the aquarium hobby came from the Americas, but Africa now has to be given credit as the home continent of a larger and larger percentage of the cichlid species available for sale to hobbyists. Both groups provide some highly colorful and interesting fishes, and both groups provide some very bad actors along with some live-and-let-lives.

Included in the American species are the "dwarf" cichlids, the ram (*Microgeophagus ramirezi*) and the *Apistogramma* and *Nannacara* species, as well as mid-sized fishes such as the angelfish and larger cichlids such as the oscar and Jack Dempsey.

All of the American cichlids are more aggressive than most of the mindless schooling fishes like the small tetras and danios, but that doesn't mean that all of them are troublemakers. They like to stake out an area of the tank and defend it as their own, and they

PHOTO BY H. J. RICHTER.

One of the most popular of the smaller cichlid species is the ram, *Microgeophagus ramirezi*, which is available in a number of different color variations, including golden; a long-finned variety also is available. Males will contest among themselves, but this species is in the main very peaceful and makes a fine choice for a beginning hobbyist who wants to get acquainted with fishes of the family Cichlidae but has only a small aquarium. The individual shown is a female, and note the ovipositor visible at her lower mid-body section: she has either just finished or just begun to spawn.

like to put on shows of bluffing and threatening, especially among themselves, but the angelfish and the ram and the apistogrammas for the most part are willing to avoid confrontations as long as they're not defending eggs or fry. The same is true of even some of the big cichlids like the oscar—but in the case of the big babies you really can't gamble too much on their good behavior, because they can do a tremendous amount of damage to other fishes when they swing into their bullying mode. The key to keeping the big cichlids peaceful is to provide them with big tanks; given enough room, they'll usually keep out of each other's way.

The bigger American cichlids generally are uprooters of plants that are rooted in the gravel of the tank, but the angelfish and the dwarfs leave plants alone.

The African cichlids fall into two main groups, the Rift Lake species and the non-Rift Lake species. The most popular non-Rift species are the kribensis (*Pelvicachromis pulcher*) and the Egyptian mouthbrooder (*Pseudocrenilabrus multicolor*), both of which are peaceful, and the jewel fish, which is a sort of Charles Manson with fins. Jewel fishes are beautiful but vicious.

PHOTO BY A. ROTH

Not fully adult but well past the juvenile stage is the oscar, *Astronotus ocellatus*, shown here. Oscars are among the larger cichlids and are very popular, one reason being that they exhibit the type of behavior that makes big cichlids in general attractive to hobbyists without being cast in the same purely homicidal mold as some of the Central American cichlids like *Herichthys dovii*. Oscars are available in a number of different color forms—red, red tiger, albino—besides the normal wild-type coloration shown here. There also is an abomination known as the long-finned oscar.

The Rift Lake cichlids come almost exclusively from Lake Malawi and Lake Tanganyika, and they have a lot to offer. First of all, some of them are among the most brightly colored fishes in the field—with their solid deep blues, yellows and oranges, they show as much over-all brightness as the platies and swordtails. Secondly, they provide almost constant action to watch. Just pile up a heap of rocks and caves in their tank and you've set the stage for an almost continuous dashing and chasing tableau as they skitter around, above and through the jumble. If you like to see a group of fishes in perpetual motion different from the back-and-forth pacing of a school of neon tetras or zebra

Pterophyllum scalare, the angelfish, is a true aquarium aristocrat. Not brightly colored (although a golden variety exists) but beautifully graceful and elegant, angelfish are long-time aquarium favorites. Angelfish exist in many different color and finnage varieties, including some really motley offshoots, but the basic body outline of the species and its proud carriage give it a style all its own. The angels pictured are veiltails of the normal (wild-type) color pattern.

Colorful without question and murderous without doubt is the beautiful but nutso jewel cichlid. The jewel cichlid shown here surrounded by its fry is of the species now designated as *Hemichromis lifalilli*, a very close relative of the fish (*Hemichromis guttatus*, formerly known in aquarium literature as *H. bimaculatus*) that was the first species called the jewel cichlid; *H. lifallili* shows much more red than *H.guttatus* both in and out of spawning condition. Whatever their degree of red coloration, jewel cichlids are very aggressive, and they're capable of dispatching even considerably larger species through constant hounding.

PHOTO BY H. J. RICHTER.

PHOTOS BY HERBERT R. AXELROD.

ABOVE: A male *Labeotropheus trewavasae*, from Africa's Lake Malawi, one of the big lakes (another is Lake Tanganyika) in Africa's Rift Valley that have provided scores of popular and semi-popular aquarium species. Kept under the proper conditions—which means, essentially, that their tank should contain an agglomeration of rocky rubble into which they can dart and dive and that their water should be very hard and alkaline and kept at around 78 degrees F.— they are seemingly always on the move, always providing some type of motion to watch, some kind of interesting action. BELOW: a pair of *Pseudotropheus lombardoi*, another cichlid species from Lake Malawi. The bright yellow male is easily distinguished from the bluish female.

An albino male *Pelvicachromis pulcher*. Commonly known as the kribensis (from its older scientific name of *Pelmatochromis kribensis*) this relatively peaceful African cichlid is from West Africa, not from any of the lakes in the Rift Valley. It's not a mouthbrooder, but it's easy to propagate, and during spawning the female of the normal color variety is very colorful.

A male *Neolamprologus brichardi*, one of the cichlids from Lake Tanganyika. The popular cichlids from Lake Tanganyika are not mouthbrooders, but they share in their Malawian cousins' fondness for hard, alkaline water and rocky substrates in their tanks. In the main less brightly colored than the popular Malawi cichlids, the Tanganyika cichlids also are less restive.

danios, get yourself some Malawi cichlids and settle back to be entertained. Just be prepared to take a few casualties from time to time, as a few of these fishes are really mean. They want more than just the thrill of the chase; they want to be in for the kill.

The most often encountered of the Malawi cichlids are *Pseudotropheus lombardoi,*

store. The popular Malawi cichlids are mouthbrooders; after the eggs are laid, one of the parents— almost always the mother—picks the eggs up in her mouth and keeps them there until the fry leave her well after hatching.

The most commonly seen of the Lake Tanganyika species are *Julidochromis marlieri, Neolamprologus leleupi* and

A male Egyptian mouthbrooder, *Pseudocrenilabrus multicolor*, with his breeding tube slightly extended. Small and not very combative against other species, this fish is the "original" African cichlid in that it was the first African cichlid species to be exported to the American and European aquarium trade.

Pseudotropheus zebra and *Labeotropheus fuelleborni.* Some of the Rift Lake fishes have many different color varieties, with fish of the same species appearing in a number of distinctly different colors and patterns, so don't be surprised if you see the same name applied to ostensibly very different fishes in a tropical fish

Neolamprologus brichardi. The species listed here are not mouthbrooders; they lay their eggs in caves and guard them there.

All of the Rift Lake cichlids like hard, alkaline water. They also like heat, so keep their temperature in the close-to-80°F range.

Male *Julidochromis marlieri*, from Lake Tanganyika, are more territory-minded than the other *Julidochromis* species. The dominant male will lord it over all other males in the tank, which is a good reason not to have more than one adult male in a tank unless it's a large tank suitably strewn with rocky interstices into which lesser males may retreat.

A male of one of the numerous color variants of *Pseudotropheus zebra*, from Lake Malawi. This species represents a wide range of possible colors and color combinations, all of which exist in the wild and are not man-made varieties. Like the other popular Lake Malawi species, especially the *Labeotropheus* species, *P. zebra* should be provided with plenty of vegetable matter in its diet.

A male of the Lake Tanganyika species *Neolamprologus leleupi*.

PHOTO BY H. J. RICHTER.

THE CHARACOIDS

The characoid (actually characiform) fishes constitute more than just one family. They constitute an order comprising about 15 different families; the family with the greatest number of species represented in aquarists' tanks is the family Characidae, the family of "true" characins, or tetras.

The family Characidae used to contain many more species than it does today. But in the 1960s and 1970s scientists broke the family down into about 15 smaller families that included both South and North American and African genera. The piranhas and silver dollars are a subfamily, Serrasalmidae. The hatchetfishes (Gasteropelicinae), pencilfishes (Lebiasinidae), and headstanders (Anostomidae) now have been split off, as have some much less frequently seen species once included among the Characidae.

PHOTO BY R. ZUKAL.

Hemigrammus ocellifer, the head-and-tail-light tetra. Inoffensive and easy to care for, this fish and the other popular small tetras such as the cardinal and neon tetras are good choices for beginning aquarists for housing in a "community" aquarium in which a number of species get along without trying to kill one another.

schooling fishes that add color and movement and not much else to a tank. Back and forth, back and forth, up and down—no wonder they say that tropical fishes are soothing to watch. Most of the tetras are better than soothing; they're stupefying. Spend an hour watching a tankful of small tetras and you'll have to get your eyes refocused.

But some of them are very colorful, and others are nicely shaped, and in the main they behave themselves well, so they've always found a home in aquarists' tanks. The most popular of them—the cardinal tetra (*Paracheirodon axelrodi*), neon tetra (*Paracheirodon innesi*) and the small elongated tetras of the genera *Hyphessobrycon* and *Hemigrammus*—are completely peaceful, but the higher-bodied *Hyphessobrycon* species, especially those with much red in their coloring, can be nippy. The latter fishes are among the most colorful and interesting of the tetras.

Tetras

In general, the tetras are small

PHOTO BY MP. AND C.PIEDNOIR

Brightly colored and very lively, the cardinal tetra is regarded by many as the class of the tetra group—and there's no gainsaying the fact that the sight of a large group of cardinals flitting in unison through a well planted aquarium is exactly the kind of thing that has caused many people to become tropical fish hobbyists. And if you think that a school of *Paracheirodon axelrodi* looks good viewed from the side as they are here, do yourself a favor and look down from *above* such a school if you get a chance; the electric-blue flashes will hypnotize you.

Regarded as the most colorful of the available tetras until the cardinal tetra arrived on the scene, the neon tetra, *Paracheirodon innesi*, is a little smaller than the cardinal tetra and a little less colorful, but it shares all of the cardinal tetra's other good points.

Other popular tetras are: the black tetra (*Gymnocorymbus ternetzi*), the bloodfin (*Aphyocharax anisitsi*), and the penguins or hockey sticks, *Thayeria boehlkei* and *Thayeria obliqua*. There are many more.

Most of the tetras make good community tank fishes. They look good and are easy to care for, and they usually don't go looking for trouble, although they take a passing nip or two at the flowing fins of slower-moving species. They don't require excessively high temperatures and readily

Black tetras (*Gymnocorymbus ternetzi*) are somber in comparison to most other popular tetra species and are a little nippier besides, but they're a very hardy fish and make a nice counterpoint to their flashier cousins in a large, well planted tank. This is a fully mature egg-laden female of the species.

Sold under the names penguin tetra and hockey stick tetra, *Thayeria boehlkei* while young is one of the more plainly colored of the tetras, but when fully adult and in good color it exhibits a very attractive iridescent green line bordering the black stripe.Whatever its age, it is a peaceful and undemanding species.

accept all types of prepared foods, even though they of course prefer live foods. Hobbyists are often advised to soften and acidify water in which they intend to keep tetras, but fiddling with the chemistry of their water shouldn't really be necessary unless you intend to spawn them.

The spawning pattern followed by characins calls for the scattering and fertilizing of the eggs, generally among bushy plants, after a lot of chasing, posturing and quivering of the parents at various places throughout the spawning tank. The fry are small and much less easy to feed than the fry of cichlids, say, but they grow quickly if given the tiny foods they need. Very few aquarists in the United States and Great Britain attempt to spawn any of the characins.

PHOTO BY R. ZUKAL.

Aphyocharax anisitsi, the bloodfin.

Hemigrammus caudovittatus, the tetra from Buenos Aires, grows larger than most other aquarium tetra species and is not loath to use its mouth in sniping attacks on its tankmates; It also feeds on aquarium plants.

PHOTO BY MP. AND C. PIEDNOIR.

A male bleeding heart tetra, *Hyphessobrycon erythrostigma*, a truly showy fish at full size and in good condition.

PHOTO BY MP. AND C. PIEDNOIR.

Gasteropelecus sternicla, one of the hatchetfishes—a group that may not be very colorful but never makes trouble.

OTHER CHARACOID FISHES

HATCHETFISHES (family Gasteropelicidae): The hatchetfishes are oddly shaped— they seem to be made up 90% of chest area—small, drab fishes that never fight with anybody and spend almost all of their time scooting around just under the surface of the water looking for small floating pieces of food. They are interesting oddities; in the wild they can get up a head of steam and "fly" out of the water for four or five yards, which is a nice trick for a small fish.

PENCILFISHES (family Lebiasinidae): The genus

Nannostomus beckfordi, a nice tankmate for other harmless small characoids. This is a male; the female would show much less red in the fins and be rounder in the belly.

Nannostomus provides a few attractive, hardy, peaceful fishes, some of which are relatively very long and thin, giving rise to the "pencilfish" name. The two species of the subgenus *Poecilobrycon* in best supply swim on the oblique, with their heads at a higher level than their tails. This is an exact

Anostomus anostomus, the striped headstander.

reversal of the habit of some of the fishes of the characoid family Anostomidae, which swim head downward and at a much greater angle of decline than the *Poecilobrycon* species have as an incline.

None of the pencilfishes does well if forced into proximity with roughhousers; they can't take the commotion and soon lose interest in food.

PIRANHAS AND SILVER DOLLARS (subfamily Serrasalminae): I've never understood the attraction of the fishes in this group, either the plant-eating *Metynnis* and *Myleus* species or the flesh-eating piranhas, *Serrasalmus*, but there is no question that people want them. They provide plenty of flash in an aquarium, what with their fast swimming and their silvery reflective scales on very deep bodies, and, of course, the piranhas come loaded with the romance of danger. They also are noticed; it's hard to miss even a half-grown *Metynnis*

Distichodus affinis, the silver distichodus, one of the few African tetras occasionally on the market. Not for beginners.

The piranha *Serrasalmus gibbus*.

anostomid swims head down and although other families of characoids contain species that are commonly called headstanders) derive their common name from their habit of keeping their heads pointed downward and their tails upward. They are attractive, but they're not good fishes for beginners, one reason being their large size as adults.

flitting through a tank, and the choppers on a piranha can keep eyes riveted. But apart from that they are mostly dull. None of the fishes in this family is a good fish for beginners.

AFRICAN TETRAS (families Citharinidae and Distichodontidae) include some very good-looking, flashily iridescent fishes, such as the Congo tetra and its close relatives, all of which are big-scaled and very reflective of light if kept in the proper surroundings.

HEADSTANDERS (family Anostomidae, although not every

A pair of *Phenacogrammus interruptus*, the Congo tetra; the male is the lower fish. Tremendously showy in large groups In large tanks, but not a good species for beginners.

THE ANABANTOIDS

Here is another group that used to be thought of as one family but now is broken down into a number of families. The anabantoids collectively are called labyrinth fishes because they come equipped with a maze-like respiratory organ that serves as an accessory to their gills. The labyrinth allows the anabantoids to "breathe" atmospheric oxygen to a certain limited degree, thereby lessening the danger of their suffocating in oxygen-poor water.

The most popular and commonly available of the anabantoids are the Siamese fighting fish, or betta, *Betta splendens* (family Belontiidae), and the various gouramis of the genera *Colisa* and *Trichogaster* (family Osphronemidae).

The Siamese fighting fish has many advantages: the males are beautiful, having long, graceful fins and being obtainable in various bright colors. They are very interesting, and the males can easily be coaxed —by letting them see at close range another male or their own image in a mirror—into

PHOTO BY K. TANAKA.

A male Siamese fighting fish, *Betta splendens*, just starting to go into his threatening mode against a rival male.

putting on a wonderful fin-spreading, gill cover-flaring, threatening display. Additionally, they can be kept in very small containers, they're easy to spawn, and their spawning routine is fascinating to observe. Their only disadvantage is that you have to keep the males separated from one another, so you can't put more than one male into the same tank.

Betta splendens and the other anabantoids discussed here, but not all other anabantoids, are bubblenesters. They construct a floating nest made of "bubbles" that they've spit out of their mouths, and into this nest they place their eggs. The male tends the eggs and later (if he doesn't eat them) the fry for a while. It's fascinating to watch a betta or gourami courtship/spawning ritual from start to finish.

There are two basic gourami groups: the small gouramis of the genus *Colisa* and the much larger gouramis of the genus *Trichogaster*. *Colisa lalia*, the dwarf gourami, is a very colorful (the males, anyway) and peaceful fish as easy to coax into spawning as the betta. It has a dwarfier relative, *Colisa chuna*, the honey dwarf gourami, that also is peaceful and easy to spawn.

Trichogaster gives us the blue, or three-spot, gourami, *Trichogaster trichopterus*, in its various color forms, including golden. Considerably larger than its *Colisa* cousins, the blue gourami also can be considerably less peaceful. But it's a very hardy and attractive, active species, not at all a bad choice for a community tank before it reaches full size. Again, this is an easy fish to coax into spawning, and large parents can produce literally thousands of fry. Much more sedate is the pearl gourami, *Trichogaster leeri*. The pearl gourami is less hardy than the blue gourami and also is less easy to spawn—but it's a beauty, and it behaves itself better than the blue. A very classy fish, but it won't do well if maintained with frenetic companions.

Two other *Trichogaster* species, *T. microlepis*, the moonlight gourami, and *T. pectoralis*, the snakeskin gourami, appear occasionally. I wouldn't give tank space to either of them. Nor would I to another fish with "gourami" in its name, the kissing gourami, *Helostoma temmincki* (family Helostomatidae). This fish gets a lot of ink because of its habit of "kissing"—opening its mouth wide and then plastering it onto another kissing gourami's open mouth, or onto the side of the tank or a rock or the side of another fish, whichever presents itself first. The kissing gourami comes in two color forms: the cultivated whitish pink

PHOTO BY H. J. RICHTER.

Male dwarf gourami, *Colisa lalia*, of the original color variety.

PHOTO BY MP. AND C. PIEDNOIR.

Gold color variety of *Trichogaster trichopterus*.

Moonlight gourami, also called moonbeam gourami, *Trichogaster microlepis*.

PHOTO BY MP. AND C. PIEDNOIR

Male snakeskin gourami, *Trichogaster pectoralis.*

A male pearl gourami, *Trichogaster leeri*, tending his bubblenest. As with other *Trichogaster* species, the adult male can be distinguished from the adult female by his longer dorsal fin and richer coloration.

and the wild green form. With luck, you'll never see the green form.

The anabantoids have the distinction of giving the hobby what I consider far and away the hardiest aquarium fish ever seen. This honor has to go to the paradise fish, *Macropodus opercularis*; this good-looking but aggressive species can take just about anything an unthinking beginner can dish out by way of aquarium mismanagement. I mean, here's a fish that hangs in there. Warm water/cold water, soft water/hard water, acid water/alkaline water, low water/high water, who cares? The paradise fish takes it all and comes back for more. And it comes in two color varieties: wild form, a sort of reddish and blue, and albino. Too bad it's mean.

The more common pinkish/whitish color variety of the kissing gourami, *Helostoma temmincki.*

Male blue gourami, *Trichogaster trichopterus.*

Male paradise fish of the wild-type (that is, non-albino) color under his bubblenest.

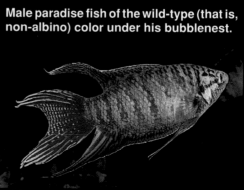

FAMILY CYPRINIDAE

The family Cyprinidae is a big family that contains many aquarium species, from the goldfish through the "sharks." Having now mentioned goldfish, let's dismiss them (and their friends the koi with them), as they're not fit topics for discussion in a book dealing with real tropical fish.

For aquarium purposes, the family Cyprinidae contains three main groups: the barbs, the danios/rasboras and the labeos. Most of the fishes in the first two groups are small, non-belligerent species that offer aquarists good looks, ease of maintenance and plenty of movement. The labeos are bigger and less active cyprinids; they provide the hobbyist with more problems but offer much more in terms of personality.

Cyrinids in the main require cooler water than the purely tropical species like some of the anabantoids, and they should have plenty of free room in which to swim. They take all kinds of prepared foods with no hesitation at all, and they usually get along with all of their tankmates. The most common method of breeding among them is simply to scatter eggs either at random or into bunches of plants anchored or floating in the tank. The eggs of some species are adhesive or at least semi-adhesive and stick where they're scattered, and the

PHOTO BY MP. AND C. PIEDNOIR.

A group of semi-longfinned rosy barbs, *Puntius conchonius*.

PHOTO BY A. ROTH.

Cherry barbs, *Puntius titteya*, among the smallest of the commonly available barb species.

Gold barbs, *Puntius semifasciolatus*.

PHOTO BY MP. AND C. PIEDNOIR.

The male in this pair of black ruby barbs, *Puntius nigrofasciatus*, has enhanced coloring and is actively courting the female.

eggs of others have no stickiness at all and just lie where they fall.

Among the barbs are the very popular tiger barb (*Puntius tetrazona*), rosy barb (*Puntius conchonius*), cherry barb (*Puntius titteya*) and golden barb (*Puntius semifasciolatus*). Another popular barb is the tinfoil barb, *Puntius schwanenfeldi*, which is usually offered for sale at a small size but is capable, as an adult, of making most of the other barbs look like midgets.

The class of the field is the tiger barb, a crisply marked, colorful fish that's always on the move. Tiger barbs are "action" fishes; whatever they're doing they do it fast. If you want to see how a school of piranhas attacks its prey without going to the expense of setting up an aquarium to house a school of piranhas, get a school of tiger barbs: they'll hit food the same way. Snap, snap, snap, it's gone. Live foods, flakes, pellets, granules, frozen chunks, it doesn't matter—they'll hit it and love it, and you'll love watching them. Tiger barbs have a reputation as nibblers of the fins of slower-moving long-finned

fishes such as angelfish and bettas. The way to avoid having them nip other fishes is to make sure that there are enough tiger barbs in the tank to keep each other busy.

The other barbs share in the tiger barb's quick-paced style but don't have quite the zest for life the tiger barb shows, although the rosy barb comes fairly close. In good condition, incidentally, the male rosy barb takes on a purplish-red color over its entire body; between its bright color and its large, reflective scales, it becomes a very showy specimen.

The danios are smaller and comparatively longer-bodied than the barbs, but they exhibit the same restless, fast-swimming back and forth pacing of the tank. As a matter of fact, they're even faster and more restless than the barbs. A tankful of tetras can lull you to sleep with their continuous back and forth patrolling, but the danios will give you eyestrain trying to keep up with them.

The most common danio is the zebra danio, *Brachydanio rerio*. This small—usually only an inch to inch and a half—inexpensive, easy-to-breed fish is an excellent choice for a beginner. It and its

A male zebra danio, *Brachydanio rerio*. Good-looking, peaceful, non-fussy in its requirements, inexpensive, easy to breed—an all-around good fish for beginners.

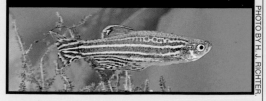

variant, the leopard danio, are peaceful and undemanding. Less suitable but still very good is the giant danio, a colorful species that by my observation has to hold the record for uninterrupted frenzied back-and-forth high-speed prancing; it just doesn't stop.

A number of different rasboras (genus *Rasbora*) are available on a sporadic basis. Most of them are very similar to the danios in habit

Rasbora heteromorpha, by the way, doesn't go in for any commonplace cyprinid egg-scattering nonsense; it attaches its eggs one by one to the underside of plant leaves.

Rivaling the zebra danio as the most common and inexpensive aquarium cyprinid (apart from the common comet goldfish, of course) is the white cloud, *Tanichthys albonubes*. White clouds are small and very hardy,

PHOTO BY H. J. RICHTER.

A group of *Rasbora heteromorpha*, an excellent community tank species.

but are larger and don't move as fast. The two most common rasboras are *Rasbora heteromorpha*, the harlequin rasbora, also called red rasbora and just plain "the rasbora," and the scissortail rasbora, *Rasbora trilineata*. The harlequin rasbora is an old-time favorite, a delicate-looking and attractive little fish that never bothers anybody; the scissortail is much bigger and relatively undistinguished.

The female of this pair of white clouds, *Tanichthys albonubes*, is very heavy with eggs.

PHOTO BY R. ZUKAL.

Bala shark (also called tricolor shark), *Balanteocheilos melanopterus*.

especially as regards being able to withstand cool water. They're peaceful and accept all foods, and they are the easiest of all egglayers to raise fry from—by which I mean that they are the only egglayers I know of that will regularly increase their population if left in a tank by themselves, with the aquarist making no effort to save the eggs or feed the fry. (It has to be a nicely planted tank without any other fishes in it, now, not some sterile prison populated by fry-glommers.)

A few species in the cyprinid genera *Labeo* and *Epalzeo-rhynchos* have the word "shark" in their common names, supposedly

Black shark, *Labeo chrysophekadion*.

because of the way their dorsal fin resembles the dorsal fin of a surface-cruising shark. *Epalzeorhynchos bicolor*, the red-tailed black shark, and *Epalzeorhynchos erythrurus*, the rainbow shark, are very popular, even though they usually look far from their best in dealers' tanks.

The sharks bully one another terribly, and keeping more than one of them in the same tank almost always guarantees constant squabbling. The dominant fish— usually, but not in every instance, the biggest—harries the others to the point of exhaustion, often death, even if plenty of good hiding places are provided in the tank in the form of caves and hollows. A fully grown red-tailed black shark is not loath to apply his bullyboy tactics to other species, either.

Another cyprinid with "shark" in its common name is the bala shark, also called tricolor shark, *Balanteocheilos melanopterus*. This

Red-tailed black shark, *Epalzeorhynchos bicolor*.

fish is much more closely related to the barbs than to the *Labeo* species, and it acts in typical barb fashion. It's a fast, flashy fish and very popular, even though it gets too big eventually for small (30 gallons and below) tanks.

THE CATFISHES

There are about 15 families of catfishes represented among the species offered for sale on the aquarium market. Most catfishes found in aquariums, though, can be traced to only two families, with two or three more families well below them in importance and the balance of the 15 families each contributing only a species or two.

The two most important families are the Callichthyidae and the Loricariidae. The callichthyid catfishes include the ubiquitous *Corydoras* catfishes, and the loricariids include the suckermouth catfishes, also called the "armored" catfishes even though they're not much more heavily armored than the callichthyids. The catfishes in these two families don't have scales; they have a sort of shingle or clapboard arrangement, with hard plates overlapping each other over wide areas of the body. Some other catfishes have no plates or scales of any kind.

On the next level of importance would be the family Pimelodidae and its long-whiskered *Pimelodus* and *Pimelodella* species, and the family Mochokidae, which provides the *Synodontis* species from Africa, some of which habitually swim upside down. The family Siluridae and its glass catfishes, genus *Kryptopterus*, rounds out the second level.

The remainder of the families give us occasional visitors like the

PHOTO BY MP. AND C. PIEDNOIR.

Corydoras ambiacus swimming in formation. This is just one of the many harmless little *Corydoras* catfishes available to hobbyists. They're not very colorful, but many are attractively patterned, and they're all interesting and tank-worthy.

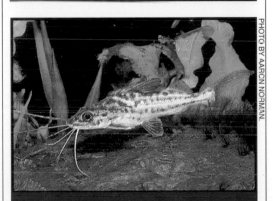

PHOTO BY AARON NORMAN.

Pimelodus clarias. Watch out for those long-whiskered catfishes!

Synodontis nigriventris; guess why it's called an upside-down catfish.

PHOTO BY DR. HERBERT R. AXELROD.

Corydoras panda.

banjo catfishes (family Aspredinidae or Bunocephalidae, depending on who's doing the classifying); doradid catfishes (family Doradidae); bullheads (family Ictaluridae); and the delightfully ugly electric catfish (family Malapteruridae).

The catfishes have many different ways to spawn. Among the callichthyid catfishes, for example, some of the popular aquarium species (*Corydoras*) go through an involved process of positioning and egg-fertilizing, the end result of which is that the female runs around the tank with

A female *Corydoras aeneus* carrying eggs clasped between her pelvic fins. *C. aeneus*, which is also available in a very attractive albino form, is the most common of all the *Corydoras* species—a true mainstay of the aquarium hobby.

eggs clasped in her ventral fins and sticks them to various places in the tank, while other species (*Callichthys* and *Hoplosternum*) are bubblenesters. Among the suckermouth catfishes, eggs are deposited in tunnel-like shelters (pieces of plastic piping serve nicely), where they are diligently tended by the male. Spawnings of species from the other families of catfishes are comparatively rare.

When choosing catfishes for your tank, keep in mind that some catfishes, even small ones, are very efficient predators. They simply go around gobbling up any fish that will fit into their mouths,

A golden color variety of one of the *Hypostomus* sucker-mouth catfishes from South America. These fish are not suited for small tanks.

and their mouths are pretty big. They do their best work in the dark, so you won't catch them at it, but don't let innocent looks fool you.

All of the *Corydoras* species are harmless, and the loricariids are not fish-gobblers either. The glass catfishes, the banjo catfishes and the upside down catfishes aren't much for wolfing down their tankmates—but beware the pimelodids, the clariids and the ictalurids. In general, if you see long whiskers on a catfish, be guided by the notion that those whiskers are there for a purpose: to help locate unwary tankmates (especially in the dark) and help funnel them into the mouth. A big bewhiskered catfish can be oh so droll in your dealer's tank, but when you take him home and discover that you've bought a combination of Godzilla and the Holland Tunnel, watch out.

Most aquarium catfishes like warm water and good shelter in their tanks. Some are strictly shy or nocturnal and hate to leave their hiding places, and they don't take kindly to being disturbed. The catfishes are basically non-picky in their choice of food, with some (the suckermouth cats are examples) appreciating soft vegetation in the diet. Many of the catfishes are very spinous and can get stuck in nets easily; when extricating them, remember that those same spines can get stuck into you easily, too.

The catfishes are a very diverse and interesting group, well worth keeping for their own sake and not because of any clean-up function they're supposed to perform in your tank. They're not the most colorful fishes around, and there are some dangerous characters among them, but in the main they're very satisfying specimens with a special charm. If you can't get to appreciate the antics of a group of *Corydoras* as they roll their movable eyes and make occasional berserk dashes to the surface for air, you might not have enough of the hobbyist in you.

PHOTO BY DR. HERBERT R. AXELROD.

Glass catfish, *Kryptopterus bicirrhis*, at their glassiest. A very interesting oddity, but a little too finicky and sedate for beginners.

PHOTO BY H. J. RICHTER.

Acanthodoras cataphractus, one of the doradid catfishes, a group that beginners can do without.

Synodontis multipunctatus, better looking than *S. nigriventris* and not an upside-down swimmer.

PHOTO BY H. J. RICHTER.

THE LOACHES

The loaches (family Cobitidae) comprise two distinctly different-looking groups: the long, worm shaped species like the kuhli loaches, and the more regular high-bodied forms like the clown loach and other *Botia* species.

The kuhli (often given as coolie) loaches are harmless, comical fishes that like to hide but lose much of their timidity and make themselves very visible in the tank if they don't feel threatened by their tankmates.

The genus *Botia* includes some very distinctively marked and colored species, the clown loach (*Botia macracantha*) being the best known and most colorful of them. Clown loaches don't normally go looking for trouble in

PHOTO BY MP. AND C. PIEDNOIR.

The clown loach, *Botia macracantha*.

their aquarium, except among themselves, but they can handle what comes their way. Like all other loaches, they have an erectible spine below the eye, and they know how to use that spine to maximum effect as a weapon.

No loach species is regularly spawned under aquarium conditions.

Pangio myersi, one of the kuhli loach species that have been favorites of tropical fish hobbyists for many years.

PHOTO BY MP AND C. PIEDNOIR.

MISCELLANEOUS FAMILIES

The families and family groups of fishes covered up to this point are the ones that provide the great bulk of species for the aquarium hobby. About a dozen other families also provide aquarium fishes, some of those fishes being rightly popular and some of them being very sensibly avoided. Those families are treated here, in no particular order.

Arowanas (Family Osteoglossidae)

You'll see baby arowanas (either the regular arowana, *Osteoglossum bicirrhosum*, or the black arowana, *Osteoglossum*

PHOTO BY H. J. RICHTER.

A very young *Osteoglossum ferreirai* with yolk sac.

ferreirai) offered for sale quite often, usually at such a young age that part of the fish's yolk sac is still attached, hanging off like loose intestines. Arowanas are interesting but grow to enormous size, and they're not easy to feed.

Rainbowfishes (Family Melanotaeniidae)

Excellent community tank fish except for the very large ones. Colorful, peaceful, hardy and easy to spawn, they scatter eggs that

PHOTO BY MP. AND C. PIEDNOIR.

The rainbowfish *Glossolepis incisus*.

hang by threads off vegetation in the tank.

Gobies (Family Gobiidae)

Much less often seen than they once were, the bumblebee gobies (*Brachygobius*) are interesting but not easy to keep. They need salt in their water and many hiding places in the tank, and they can be very picky about what they choose to eat. They're very shy, and if you provide them with the hiding places they want you might never see them.

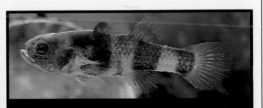

Brachygobius nunus, one of the bumblebee gobies.

Knife Fishes (Family Notopteridae, from Africa; family Apteronotidae, from South America)

Big, bizarrely shaped fishes that can be highly predatory once they put on some size, which they do

The black ghost knife fish, *Apteronotus albifrons*, is a good deal less combative and predatory than many of the other knife fishes.

quickly. Even while small they can be very quarrelsome among their own kind. Strange-looking fish, the best thing they're good for is provoking conversation.

Chinese Algae Eaters (Family Gyrinocheilidae)

The one aquarium species that this small family provides, *Gyrinocheilus aymonieri*, has become an aquarium standby, reaching almost the you-need-a-couple-of-these-to-complete-your-tank status of the *Corydoras* catfish. It is an efficient algae eater, using its ugly suction cup mouth diligently.

This species is peaceful while it's small, but as it ages and gains size and bulk it starts to get nasty, often getting into scraps with fishes much bigger than itself—and doing damage to them.

Chinese algae eater, *Gyrinocheilus aymonieri*.

If you're looking to create a little aquaristic turmoil, put a fully grown Chinese algae eater into a tank with a good-size red-tailed black shark and see what happens. The Chinese algae eater does not come from China. But then again, neither did Chinese Gordon.

Spiny Eels (Family Mastacembelidae)

These eely-looking specimens are interesting and easy to maintain, and they'll keep you amused by digging into the gravel

Mastacembelus erythrotaenia, the tire-track eel.

and poking out only their heads. They like privacy, so give them good shelter—but not too much, or you won't see them. The colorful tire-track eel, *Mastacembelus erythrotaenia*, is very popular but gets too big for most beginners' tanks. Spiny eels are great escape artists; make sure that you keep an aquarium containing a spiny eel well (and heavily) covered.

Puffers (Family Tetraodontidae)

Many people think these weirdos to be comical cuties, but to me they look evil with those bulging, staring eyes and that wicked parrot's beak of a mouth. Most puffers are bad news; don't trust them.

Closeup of the head of a mature snakehead of the genus *Channa*. For many an unwary victim, that baleful glare is the last thing they ever see.

Tetraodon schoutedeni, one of the puffers that new aquarists have a tendency to think kindly of until they put them into their tanks and see the damage they're capable of.

Snakeheads (Family Channidae)

This family has one thing going for it; you can condemn every fish in it with complete assurance that you're not wronging any of them. Killers, every one. The species most often seen is *Channa micropeltes*, which is attractively marked the length of its serpentine body with a broad red stripe to sucker the unwary. Keep the snakeheads away from your tanks.

Elephantnoses (Family Mormyridae)

Appearances deceive. The fishes in this family look decidedly stupid, but they're not. They're very interesting and fun to watch; unfortunately, they're shy and won't give you much chance to enjoy them until they're accustomed to their surroundings in your tank. They're not big fans of the prepared dried foods, but they

The elephantnose *Gnathonemus tamandua*.

avidly accept frozen foods, especially frozen bloodworms.

Killifishes (Family Cyprinodontidae)

Now you are face to face with one of the eternal mysteries of the universe: why don't you see any killifishes for sale? Killifishes are among the most beautiful/colorful/graceful/interesting of all aquarium fishes, true. And they are among the easiest to breed and raise, true. (Most killifish fry are larger than the fry of other egglaying species at hatching, so they're easier to feed.) So why aren't they more popular? Why is it that if you want one you have to join a fish club—not a bad

A male *Jordanella floridae*, native to Florida.

idea at that—or enter into correspondence to buy eggs from the chief of a West African tribe? Nobody knows; that's why it's a mystery. If you want some killifishes, you'll have a hard time finding a store that carries any, unless you're satisfied with *Jordanella floridae*, the flag fish, a killie that spawns like a cichlid. Don't settle for *Jordanella* if you can obtain any of the small African *Aphyosemion* species such as the lyretail, *Aphyosemion australe*, a delicately beautiful fish and not at all difficult to keep.

INDEX

Acanthodoras cataphractus, 59
Angelfish, 11, 32, 34, 54
Anostomus anostomus, 48
Aphyocharax anisitsi, 47
Aphyocharax rubripinnis, 46
Aphyosemion australe, 13, 64
Apistogramma, 32, 34
Apteronotus albifrons, 62
Arowana, 61
Astronotus ocellatus, 34
Badis badis, 12
Bala Shark, 56
Balanteocheilos melanopterus, 56
Balloon Molly, 30
Banjo Catfish, 58
Barbs, 11, 53-54
Betta splendens, 8, 50
Black Arowana, 61
Black Ghost Knife Fish, 62
Black Molly, 31
Black Neon Tetra, 10
Black Shark, 56
Bleeding Heart Tetra, 47
Bloodfin, 46-47
Blue Gourami, 51-52
Botia macracantha, 60
Brachydanio rerio, 54
Brachygobius nunus, 61
Bumblebee Goby, 61
Callichthys, 58
Cardinal Tetra, 11, 44-46
Chameleon Fish, 12
Channa micropeltos, 4, 64
Channa, 63
Cherry Barb, 53-54
Chinese Algae Eater, 62
Cichlids, 11, 32-43
Clown Loach, 60
Colisa chuna, 51
Colisa lalia, 50-51
Colisa, 50
Congo Tetra, 49
Coolie Loach, 60
Corydoras acutus, 16
Corydoras aeneus, 58
Corydoras ambiacus, 57
Corydoras panda, 58
Corydoras, 16, 57-59
Danios, 11, 40, 53-55
Distichodus affinis, 49
Dwarf Gourami, 50-51
Egyptian Mouthbrooder, 34, 40
Electric Catfish, 11, 58
Elephantnose, 64
Epalzeorhynchos bicolor, 56
Gasteropelecus sternicla, 48
Giant Danio, 55
Glass Catfish, 57-59
Glossolepis incisus, 61
Gnathonemus tamandua, 64
Gold Barb, 53-54
Goldfish, 20, 53, 55
Guppy, 2-3, 14, 16, 19-21
Gymnocorymbus ternetzi, 46
Gyrinocheilus aymonieri, 62
Harlequin Rasbora, 55
Hatchetfish, 11, 44, 48
Headstanders, 44, 48-49

Helostoma temmincki, 51
Hemichromis bimaculatus, 36
Hemichromis guttatus, 36
Hemichromis lifalilli, 36-37
Hemigrammus caudovittatus, 47
Hemigrammus ocellifer, 44
Hemigrammus, 44
Herichthys dovii, 34
Hockey Stick Tetra, 46
Honey Dwarf Gourami, 51
Hoplosternum, 58
Hyphessobrycon erythrostigma, 47
Hyphessobrycon herbertaxelrodi, 10
Hyphessobrycon, 44
Hypostomus, 58
Jack Dempsey, 32
Jewel Fish, 32, 34, 36-37
Jordanella floridae, 64
Julidochromis marlieri, 40-41
Killifish, 13, 18, 64
Kissing Gourami, 51-52
Knife Fish, 9, 61-62
Koi, 53
Kribensis, 34, 39
Kryptopterus bicirrhis, 59
Kryptopterus, 57
Kuhli Loach, 60
Labeotropheus fuelleborni, 40
Labeotropheus trewavasae, 38
Laetacara curviceps, 8
Lemon Tetra, 11
Leopard Danio, 55
Loaches, 11, 60
Lyretail, 13, 64
Macropodus opercularis, 52
Malapteruridae, 58
Malapterurus electricus, 11
Marigold Variatus Platy, 25
Mastacembelidae, 62
Mastacembelus erythrotaenia, 62
Melanotaenia maccullochi, 5
Metynnis, 48-49
Microgeophagus ramirezi, 32-33
Mollienesia, 30
Mollies, 7, 14-16, 18, 29-31
Moonlight Gourami, 51
Morulius chrysophekadion, 56
Myleus, 48-49
Nannacara, 32
Nannostomus beckfordi, 48
Neolamprologus brichardi, 39-40
Neolamprologus leleupi, 40, 42-43
Neon Tetra, 11, 34, 44, 46
Oscar, 32, 34
Osteoglossum bicirrhosum, 61
Osteoglossum ferreirai, 61
Pangio myersi, 60
Paracheirodon axelrodi, 44-45
Paracheirodon innesi, 44, 46
Paradise Fish, 52
Pearl Gourami, 51-52
Pelmatochromis kribensis, 39
Pelvicachromis pulcher, 34, 39
Pencilfish, 11, 44, 48
Penguin Tetra, 46
Phenacogrammus interruptus, 49

Pimelodella, 57
Pimelodus clarias, 57
Piranha, 44, 48, 54
Platies, 14-16, 18, 21-27, 34
Poecilia latipinna, 29
Poecilia reticulata, 20
Poecilia sphenops, 14, 29
Poecilia velifera, 17, 29
Poecilobrycon, 48
Psedotropheus zebra, 40-41
Pseudocrenilabrus multicolor, 34, 40
Pseudotropheus lombardoi, 38, 40
Pterophyllum scalare, 35
Puffers, 62
Puntius conchonius, 53-54
Puntius nigrofasciatus, 54
Puntius schwanenfeldi, 54
Puntius semifasciolatus, 53-54
Puntius tetrazona, 54
Puntius titteya, 53-54
Rainbow Shark, 56
Rainbowfish, 5, 11, 61
Ram, 32-34
Rasbora heteromorpha, 55
Rasbora trilineata, 55
Red Delta Guppy, 19
Red Rasbora, 55
Red-lined Snakehead, 4
Red-tailed Black Shark, 56
Rosy Barb, 53-54
Sailfin Molly, 3, 14, 17
Scissortail Rasbora, 55
Serrasalmus gibbus, 49
Siamese Fighting Fish, 8, 11, 50
Silver Distichodus, 49
Silver Dollar, 44, 48
Snakehead, 63-64
Snakeskin Gourami, 51-52
Spiny Eel, 11, 62
Suckermouth Catfish, 57-59
Swordtail, 3, 14, 16, 18, 21, 23, 26-28, 34
Synodontis multipunctatus, 59
Synodontis nigriventris, 57, 59
Tanichthys albonubes, 55
Tetraodon schoutedeni, 64
Tetras, 11, 44-47, 54
Thayeria boehlkei, 46
Thayeria obliquua, 46
Tiger Barb, 54
Tinfoil Barb, 54
Tire-track Eel, 62
Trichogaster leeri, 51-52
Trichogaster microlepis, 51
Trichogaster pectoralis, 51-52
Trichogaster trichopterus, 51-52
Tricolor Shark, 56
Upside-down Catfish, 57-58
White Cloud, 55
Xenomystus nigri, 9
Xenotoca eiseni, 18
Xiphophorus helleri, 26
Xiphophorus variatus, 15, 21-23
Xipophorus maculatus, 21-23
Zebra Danio, 40, 54-55